YOUR KNOWLEDGE HAS VALUE

- - We will publish your bachelor's and master's thesis, essays and papers

- - Your own eBook and book - sold worldwide in all relevant shops

- - Earn money with each sale

Upload your text at www.GRIN.com and publish for free

Michael Kulüke

Racism And Racial Theories in V.S. Naipaul's 'Half A Life'

GRIN Verlag

Bibliografische Information der Deutschen Nationalbibliothek:

Die Deutsche Bibliothek verzeichnet diese Publikation in der Deutschen National-
bibliografie; detaillierte bibliografische Daten sind im Internet über http://dnb.d-
nb.de/ abrufbar.

Imprint:

Copyright © 2008 GRIN Verlag GmbH
Druck und Bindung: Books on Demand GmbH, Norderstedt Germany
ISBN: 978-3-656-41365-3

GRIN - Your knowledge has value

Der GRIN Verlag publiziert seit 1998 wissenschaftliche Arbeiten von Studenten, Hochschullehrern und anderen Akademikern als eBook und gedrucktes Buch. Die Verlagswebsite www.grin.com ist die ideale Plattform zur Veröffentlichung von Hausarbeiten, Abschlussarbeiten, wissenschaftlichen Aufsätzen, Dissertationen und Fachbüchern.

Visit us on the internet:

http://www.grin.com/

http://www.facebook.com/grincom

http://www.twitter.com/grin_com

Hausarbeit

Michael Kulüke

WS 2007/2008

Racism And Racial Theories in V.S. Naipaul's

'Half A Life'

Inhaltsverzeichnis

1. General introduction

1.1. The Writer

Vidiadhar Surajprasad Naipaul was born on August, 17th 1932 in Chaguanas, a city in Trinidad and Tobago, as a descendant of a Indian immigrant to the country.

Later on he lived in Port Of Spain with his family, where he attented The Queens College. Due to a scholarship, which he won, he was able to study in Oxford, England.

After his studies he worked as an editor at the BBC for the "Carribbean Voices" project, and later on as an editor for various departments.

His first novel was "This Mystic Masseur", a story which is later on meant sarcastical by most reviewers.

With the possibility of viewing his own native origin from a wider distance, he put more and more detail in his works, which reflected happenings in post-colonial circumstances in mostly satirical ways. Naipaul begins to travel a lot in the 1960s, and processes his impressions within his novels, which are mostly fictional, but also partly autobiographic and in form of reports about his trips. The places where his stories take place are not bound to his personal origin, but to a various amount of global locations which appear to have been affected by international colonisation.

His theories about post-colonial society and the struggling of the descendants in post-colonial environments were widely respected from the instant they were published, and some of the aspects his books were written about have been recognised as almost prophetical. He also investigates the social mechanisms between colonised societies and the former colonisers, which affect the people decades after the official end of superiority of the colonisers. Often neglected as a "travel reporter", his reports are far more content of academic and non-academic observations, which make his stories interesting for valuers of social sciences, and for people who just travel a lot.

1.2. The Book

"Half A Life" has had its debut on October 16th, 200, just a few days after its author was awarded with the Nobel Prize of Literature.

The novel is about the struggle of Willie Somerset Chandran to find his own identity in a world minted by post-colonial breaks in society and politics.

His father, a Brahmin, is described as a person who went through his life by outer influences, and sparsely by own intention, what ends up in a marriage with a woman whom he does not love nor respect.

After knowing the reason for being named Somerset, as his father told him, he leaves with a significant urge his origin to make up a new life in London, England.

After years of studying, and encounters with different personalities of more or less multicultural background, he recognises the urge to write, to process his inner unease about his origin and the perceptions of the 'modern' world in which he lives at that moment.

Some struggles with the clash of cultures later, which had social, economical and sexual paragraphs, he meets the East-African girl Ana, who has mixed cultural backgrounds.

After a while he decides to go to her country, an unknown Portuguese colony in eastern Africa.

The main concern in the next eighteen years is to overcome his own rudimentary understanding of sexual desire and process with under aged prostitutes or an affair with a woman of the town. He severely observes the break in the history of that country with the last struggles of official Portuguese government and the waiting liberation movement incorporated by the guerilla.

In the last paragraphs of his life there he recognises that his life in Africa is far from what his own life should be, and he leaves Ana, after betraying her for years, for good.

2. Racism and a reference to (post-)colonialism

2.1. A definition of racism

Racism is a cultural phenomenon which appears in broader communities of the same ethnicity or in smaller groups of people with apparently the same physical attributes. It suggests that human beings can be divided into groups and standards of similar or equal attributes and characteristics and so enables several social and cultural consequences and several ideologies whose basic arguments depend on the set-up of a natural or cultural human hierarchy.

The terms of this classification are mostly biological, but also of a cultural (religious, linguistic and general cultural differences) base.

The definition of racism are of various kinds and keep a whole set of social scientists busy, but the basic terms are after thousands of years of racism almost clear outlined.

Albert Memmi was able to outline the various characteristics of racism and its influence on human characters in both a more extreme and a recessive way:

"Es gibt zweifelsohne den Rassisten im engeren Sinne des Wortes, der unter Berufung auf biologische Unterschiede den anderen unterdrückt und daraus seinen Nutzen zieht; der überzeugt ist, diese unterschiedlichen Merkemale ließen sich zu kohärenten Bündeln zusammenfassen, die er als Rassen bezeichnet – [...] Aber ebenso unstreitig gibt es den Rassisten im weiteren Sinne - [...] - der die biologischen Unterschiede möglicherweise auch sieht, sie jedoch nicht zur Grundlage seiner Beschuldigungen macht."[1]

Both forms of racism have the same consequence: violent and verbal aggression, and a definitive revaluation of the most inner self on someone else's account.

Race itself is best defined by Ashcroft, Griffiths and Tiffin in their work 'Post-Colonial Studies: The Key Concepts':

"'Race' is a term for the classification of human beings into physically, biologically and genetically distinct groups. The notion of race assumes, firstly, that humanity is divided into unchanging natural types, recognizable by physical

---

[1] Memmi, Albert, Rassismus, S. 97, Hamburg 1992

features that are transmitted 'through the blood' and permit distinctions to be made between 'pure' and 'mixed' races. Furthermore, the term implies that the mental and moral behaviour of human beings, as well as individual personality, ideas and capacities, can be related to racial origin, and that knowledge of that origin provides a satisfactory account of the behaviour."[2]

2.2. Racism and Colonialism

Both terms stand in a close relation to each other. The feeling of superiority of the first colonizers towards the native population was founded on the biological and cultural differences between them, and so the pure and definitive argumentation for a racial segregation between the colonisers, who themselves found to be in a superior state of both culture and god-given nature, and the colonised, who were suppressed through the ways of modern armoury with few chances to emancipate themselves and to defend their own privileges in their native origin.

"By translating the fact of colonial oppression into a justifying theory, however spurious, European race thinking initiated a hierarchy of human variation that has been difficult to dislodge. Although race is not specifically an invention of imperialism, it quickly became on of imperialism's most supportive ideas [...]"[3]
Colonialism and the attitude towards the colonised people often refer directly to the definition of racism as a tool of segregation, revaluation and suppression without establishing a logical and rational system of argument towards the own and foreign people.

That colonialism must not be understood as a proceeding from European powers towards the so called underdeveloped countries with natural resources not being given in the Mother countries should be clear. Racial differences were not centred on obvious differences like skin, but also on apparently smaller differences like regional language and traditions. So the Irish were targeted by a large campaign of English racism in the outgoing 17th and 18th century, as also the people of eastern Europe, as well as the Russians, were neglected by the

---

[2] Ashcroft, Bill, Griffiths, Gareth, Tiffin, Hellen, Post-Colonial Studies: The Key Concepts, S.198, Abingdon 2000
[3] Ashcroft, Bill, Griffiths, Gareth, Tiffin, Hellen, Post-Colonial Studies: The Key Concepts, S.198, Abingdon 2000

'superior' countries and people of Central-Europe, which proceeded until the catastrophe of the second world war.

Colonisation and racism with their uprooting effects are widely recognised by human sciences, and the results scientists came to are quite different in their details.
As Ania Loomba says:
"Several critics, and most notably Homi K. Bhabha, have emphasised the failure of colonial discourses to produce stable and fixed identities, and suggested that cross-overs of various sorts or 'hybridity' and 'ambivalence' more adequately describe the dynamics of the colonial encounter."[4]
It is said that natives born in colonised countries have the more problems to cope with the affection of both the modern world with its omnipresent and apparently superior latitudes, but also with the traditions and values of their ancestry, which were hundreds of years faithful guides through the miseries of human lives. The prospect seen on a human identity cannot be weighted too lightly, the anchors set for a human being and its identity, also used by the colonisers to avoid identification with inferior cultures, may be struck out of the cultural ground they fit in, and hang lose with fatal consequences for the colonised, as seen in probably every region with a history of colonisation.

---

[4]Loomba, Ania, Colonialism/Postcolonialism, S. 105, London 1998

3. Willie Somerset Chandran and the Racism in 'Half A Life'

3.1. Textual references

Racism is often quoted as have its roots in the Caste-System of India, and so it is not surprising that V.S. Naipaul has put several references to racism and racist theories, also in a less violent and more literal way, in his story to underline the rootlessness of his character in search of identity and identification.

The first reference to racism can be regarded as a simple extract of Indian ideology:

"[...]and to do the only noble thing that lay in my power, which was to marry the lowest person I could find. [...] She was small and coarse-featured, almost tribal in appearance, noticeably black, with two big top teeth that showed very white."[5]

This reference is clearly about the attitude of the Brahma-Caste that people of lower caste are clearly to be made at their physical appearance, which is quite typical for the caste-system and attitude in India of the 20th century.

Once Willie left India, racial differences get more significant to the narrator when Willie meets his later Friend Percy Cato for the first time:

"Percy was a Jamaican of mixed parentage and was more brown than black. [...] The Negro is actually recessive. [...]"[6]

As Willie asks him, what his father has worked as at the Panama Canal, he says that he had been a clerk. Willie doesn't believe that, and thinks of Percys father as a simple worker.

The most significant thing about racism and racial theories is when Roger talks to Willie about an upcoming party and the guests who would be present:

"There'll be a Negro I met in West Africa when I did my National Service. He is the son of a West Indian who went to live in West Africa as part of the Back to Africa movement. [...] To keep my end up I said that African women were attractive. He said, "If you like the animal thing." [...] he has two ambitions. The first is to have a grandchild who will be pure white in appearance. He is half-way

[5]Naipaul, V.S., Half A Life, S. 10, London 2001
[6]Naipaul, V.S., Half A Life, S. 10, London 2001

there. He has five mulatto children, by five white women [...]."[7]

And furthermore a quote of the West African himself: *"It'll only be repeating something that happened on a large scale here a hundred and fifty years ago. In the eighteenth century there were over half a million black people in England. They've all vanished. They disappeared in the local population. They were bred out. The Negro gene is a recessive one. If this were more widely known there would be a good deal less racial feeling than there is. And a lot of that feeling is only skin deep, so to speak."*[8]

This may be regarded as a reckoning with the contemporary thesis that racial differences stay within the lineage and are always recognisable.

As the race riots in Notting Hill break out, Willie reacts as being confronted with a caste uprising, he stays as home and closes himself away, and when outside, is ashamed of his skin colour, which makes him feel uncomfortable.

"[...] and Willie felt at once threatened and ashamed. He felt people were looking at him. He felt the newspapers were about him. After this he stayed in the college and didn't go out. This kind of hiding wasn't new to him. It was what they used to do at home, when there was serious religious or caste trouble."[9]

The references about racial significance propagate at the moment Willie gets known to Ana. Her Portuguese ancestry is one of the spots Willie finds himself comfortable with, although he has serious problems coping with the identification as 'Ana's London Man'.

Willie refers to Julio as a man of mixed race, and his daughter, with whom he finds it easy to identify, being worried about her.[10]

Also the group of friends of Ana they have their Sunday's lunch with is clearly accepting him as a new part, he analyses their racial background with less dignity, and with a bit of a distant observer.

"Racially they were varied, from what looked like pure white to a deep brown."[11]

His analyses the history of Ana's family himself and makes out what has happened to her Portuguese father after returning to Africa with her half-African

[7] Naipaul, V.S., Half A Life, S. 89, London 2001
[8] Naipaul, V.S., Half A Life, S. 94, London 2001
[9] Naipaul, V.S., Half A Life, S. 109, London 2001
[10] Naipaul, V.S., Half A Life, S. 143, London 2001
[11] Naipaul, V.S., Half A Life, S. 144, London 2001

mother.

He also sees it difficult for mixed-raced people to keep themselves up in the surrounding of pure-raced Africans:

"In the very beginning, when I hadn't even known about the pleasures of living in the wilderness, I had thought that the mixed-race overseers couldn't have had much of a life, living so close to the Africans, surrendering so much of themselves."[12]

When Graca appears, Willie lays more concern in the problematic state of second-rank Portuguese, which he sees as a different kind as the one of Ana's ancestry.

When Gouveia appears, Willies comments about race get more neutral on behalf of the positivity he felt for white-coloured people in the past.

One can say that his attitude has grown more specific, and he never dares to describe himself in the way he observes other personalities.

3.2. Conclusion: Willie Chandran and his thoughts about race

Although his thoughts are full of racial theories throughout the book, Willie Chandran fails to find a spot in which he could fit himself in.

Racial theories are brought together in the whole story, and he is quite firm with the analysis of racial backgrounds of the people who surround him, but does not dare to identify himself with a single term which he is observing at the other people around him.

Although this is one of the main reasons for Willies failing identification and finding his one true self, the narrator stays steps away from the racial theories described before. The cultural significance of race is accepted as being given, and the accordance of skin colour and cultural difference is presented as a fact that might be criticised by spokesmen of the Anti-Racism-Movement. Whatever is to be said, Naipaul uses Race and Racism as a tool of describing the possibilities of identification in the book, and also of the problems of identification.

For example the riots in London, a symbol for the identification of masses with a

---

[12]Naipaul, V.S., Half A Life, S. 182, London 2001

single person (in this case Kelso, who had been killed by white teenagers), drive Willie in habits that he is used to from his time in India, and he misses the chance to go out and find himself in a surrounding that could enable himself to find his true one self.

His own capability of analysing the racial background of his friends and shuts him down to recognise his own roots and social belongings, and the dares to judge and criticise the the people in his surrounding, but fails fatally to find a spot with what he could describe himself.

One can say that Naipaul is far away from a traditional use of race and racism in this book, the biological and cultural differences which are widely used to alter someone's significance are here used as devices of (failing) identification.

Although Willie Somerset Chandran is obviously different to the others, he is far from identifying himself with this difference, and his own being as someone who does not fit into the circumstances he himself has set him in.

The racial background, as described by Marcus, whether it is cultural or biological, is every time something that has to be overcome, and that is the thinking Willie Chandran accepts for his own, but never speaks it out loud.

Racism is not explicit in this book, but an omnipresent tool of (failing) identification and classification, which makes it easy for Willie to come along with his fellows just as far as he needs to step into a new crisis.

4. Bibliography

Naipaul, V.S., Half A Life, London 2001

Miles, Robert, Racism, London 1989

Essed, Philomena, Goldberg, David Theo [Edt.], Race Critical Theories, Malden 2002

Loomba, Ania, Colonialism/Postcolonialism, London 1998

Ashcroft, Bill, Griffiths, Gareth, Tiffin, Hellen, Post-Colonial Studies: The Key Concepts, Abingdon 2000

Memmi, Albert, Rassismus, Hamburg 1992